Recipes to Ensure that Your dog Eats Healthily

The Best Cookbook for the Canine that You Love!!

Table of Contents

Introduction

Congratulations and thank you for purchasing a copy of this recipe book!

I am more than glad that you decided to buy this recipe book, because asides from the fact that this recipe book is an outstanding one that contains unique homemade dog meals, this recipe book is written from a place of experience!

Unlike other authors who might base their research on what they think dogs should eat, the premise of this recipe book is based on true life experiences with dogs!

I have three dogs presently: a German Shepherd, a Labrador Retriever, and a Chihuahua; all three different breeds of dogs that I have tried these recipes on and found that they really work to boost dog's health and wellbeing!!

So, if I say that the recipes in this cookbook suit every and any breed of dogs, it is the nothing short of the truth!! Regardless of the breed of your dog, you can effortlessly prepare these recipes for them, and they would love you more for it!!!

Also, this recipe book will help teach you what is good for your dog, what your dog needs to stay healthy? How much food is enough for your dog and so much more!!!

So, welcome to a new dispensation of homemade dog cooking as we flip the page to unveil our first dog recipe!!

Chapter 1 – Treat Yo' Pup: Homemade Dog Treats

1. Bacon, Peanut Butter, and Banana Dog Treats

Serving: 18 to 20 treats

Prep Time: 10 minutes

Bake Time: 20 minutes

Total Time: 30 minutes

The list of ingredients:

- 1/2 cup water
- 1 peeled banana
- 1 large egg
- 1/3 cup smooth peanut butter
- 1 cup oat flour
- 1/2 cup oats
- 1 tablespoon bacon fat, saved from the cooked bacon
- 1 tablespoon dried parsley
- 3 bacon slices (cooked and crumbled)
- 1 cup whole wheat white flour

Methods:

A. Preheat oven to 350 degrees. Line the bottom of a baking sheet with parchment paper. Set to the side for the moment.

B. Mix the oats, parsley, oat flour, and whole wheat white flour together in a mixing bowl.

C. Mash the banana in a microwave-safe bowl. Stir in

the bacon fat and the peanut butter. Place the bowl in the microwave and heat for 30 seconds. Stir the mixture and heat in the microwave for an additional 30 seconds. Keep repeating this process until the mixture is melted and smooth.

D. Let the heated mixture cool just slightly before whisking in the egg and folding in the cooked bacon.

E. Combine the wet ingredients into the dry ingredients until well combined. Slowly mix in the water, a little at a time, until the mixture has a smooth consistency.

F. Turn the dough out and onto a floured surface. Roll the dough out to a thickness of about ¼-inch.

G. Cut the dough out using the desired cookie cutter and place on the prepared baking sheet from Step 1.

H. Bake in the preheated oven for 18 to 20 minutes. Once the treats have a golden brown color, remove them from the oven and transfer to a cooling rack.

I. Store the completely cooked treats in an airtight container.

2. Baby Food Dog Biscuits

Serving: varies depending on the cookie cutter

Prep Time: 5 minutes

Bake Time: 20 minutes

Total Time: 25 minutes

The list of ingredients:

- 2 jars chicken baby food

- 2 ½ cups baby oatmeal cereal
- 2 jars carrot and sweet potato baby food

Methods:

A. Preheat oven to 350-degrees. Line the bottom of a baking sheet with parchment paper. Set to the side for the moment.

B. Mix all three ingredients together to form a sticky dough.

C. Place the dough on a floured surface and roll out to a thickness of about ¼-inch.

D. Use a cookie cutter to cut out the dough. Place the uncooked treats on the prepared baking sheet from Step 1.

E. Bake the biscuits in the preheated oven for 20 minutes. After the allotted time, remove the baking sheet from the oven.

F. Transfer the dog biscuits to a cooling rack and let cool completely before continuing.

G. Store the dog biscuits in the fridge an airtight container.

3. Apple Pumpkin Dog Treats

Serving: varies on the size and shape of the cookie cutter used

Prep Time: 5 to 10 minutes

Bake Time: 12 to 15 minutes

Total Time: 17 to 25 minutes

The list of ingredients:

- 1 large egg (lightly beaten)
- 1 medium apple
- 1 cup canned pumpkin
- 4 cups oatmeal

Methods:

A. Preheat oven to 400 degrees. Line a baking sheet with parchment paper and set to the side for the moment.

B. Pulse the oatmeal in a food processor until it has a flour-like consistency. Pour the ground oatmeal into a mixing bowl.

C. Core the apple, making sure to remove all the seeds, and grate. Place the grated apple into the mixing bowl from Step 2.

D. Mix the pumpkin and egg into the mixture. The dough will have a sticky texture.

E. Dust a flat surface with some oatmeal. Lay the dough out on the surface and roll to a thickness of about ½-inch.

F. Use a cookie cutter to cut the dough into the desired

shape and then place on the prepared baking sheet.

G. Bake the dough in the preheated oven for 12 to 15 minutes. The treats should be crispy and golden.

H. Remove the baking sheet from the oven and transfer on a cooling rack. Let cool completely before storing in an airtight container for up to 7 days.

4. Banana Bread Dog Treats

Serving:

Prep Time: 5 to 10 minutes

Bake Time: 35 minutes

Total Time: 40 to 45 minutes

The list of ingredients:

- 2 large eggs
- 1 tablespoon coconut oil

- 1/2 cup pumpkin puree
- 1/2 cup coconut flour
- 1 banana (peeled and mashed)
- 1 tablespoon ground flaxseed

Methods:

A. Preheat oven to 350 degrees. Line the bottom of a baking sheet with parchment paper. Set to the side for the moment.

B. Whisk the flaxseeds and coconut flour together until well combined. Set to the side for the moment.

C. Whisk the eggs, coconut oil, mashed banana, and pumpkin puree together until completely combined.

D. Combine the dry ingredients with the wet ingredients to create a thick batter.

E. Spread the batter into the prepared baking sheet from Step 1. Make sure to evenly spread the batter. Let sit for about 5 minutes.

F. Using a butter knife, create little squares in the batter by scoring it vertically and horizontally.

G. Place the baking sheet in the oven and bake for 35 minutes. After the allotted time, remove the baking sheet from the oven. Transfer the chewy dog treats to a cooling rack.

H. Carefully cut the treats along the lines you made in Step 6. Store the treats in an airtight container in the fridge.

5. Dog Chews

Serving: varies

Prep Time: 10 minutes

Bake Time: 3 hours

Total Time: 3 hours 10 minutes

The list of ingredients:

- 1-2 sweet potatoes

Methods:

A. Preheat oven to 250 degrees. Line the bottom of a cookie sheet with parchment paper. Set to the side for the moment.

B. Prepare the sweet potatoes by washing and them drying them.

C. Slice the prepared sweet potatoes lengthwise, making sure they have a width of no more than ¼ to 1/3-inch.

D. Lay the sliced sweet potatoes in a single layer on the prepared cookie sheet from Step 1.

E. Place in the preheated oven for 1 ½ hours. Remove from the oven and flip them over. Immediately place back in the oven for an additional 1 ½ hours.

F. Remove the dog chews from the oven and let cool completely before placing them in an airtight container. Store the chews in the fridge to prevent molding.

G. Tip: You can also use a dehydrator to make these all-natural homemade dog treats.

6. Carrot, Zucchini, and Spinach Dog Treats

Serving: varies depending on the cookie cutter used

Prep Time: 20 to 25 minutes

Bake Time: 25 minutes

Total Time: 45 to 50 minutes

The list of ingredients:

- 1 shredded zucchini
- 2 large eggs (lightly beaten)
- 1 cup baby spinach (roughly chopped)
- ½ cup old-fashioned oats
- 3 cups whole wheat flour
- 1 carrot (peeled and shredded)
- 1 cup pumpkin puree
- 1/4 cup smooth peanut butter

Methods:

A. Preheat oven to 350 degrees. Prepare a baking sheet by lining it with parchment paper. Set to the side for the moment.

B. Using an electric mixer, mix the peanut butter, pumpkin puree, and eggs together. Keep beating for a minute or two until the mixture is smooth and well combined.

C. Gradually add in the oats and the flour, mixing a little at a time, until you have incorporated them both into the mixture.

D. Mix in the spinach, zucchini, and carrot. Make sure to mix until just incorporated and avoid over mixing.

E. Lightly flour a flat surface you can work on. Place the dough on the floured surface and knead the dough 4 times.

F. Roll the dough out to a thickness of about ¼-inch. Using a cookie cutter, cut the dough out. Set the dough onto the prepared baking sheet.

G. Bake the dough in the preheated oven and bake for 20 to 25 minutes until the edges begin to turn a golden-brown color.

H. Remove the baking sheet out of the oven and transfer the treats to a cooling rack. Let cool completely before storing in an airtight container.

7. No Bake Dog Treats

Serving: 10 to 20 treats

Total Time: 5 to 10 minutes

The list of ingredients:

- 1 tablespoon organic honey
- 1 cup pumpkin puree
- 2 ½ cups oats, old-fashioned
- 1/2 cup smooth peanut butter
- 1 teaspoon ground cinnamon

Methods:

A. Place the peanut butter, pumpkin puree, honey, and cinnamon into a mixing bowl. Combine until well incorporated into one another.

B. Fold in the oats.

C. Using your hands, roll the mixture into small, bite-sized balls. Continue in this manner until you have rolled all the mixture into small balls.

D. Tada! You're done! Store the no-bake dog treats in the fridge in an airtight container.

8. Dog Bone Biscuit Treats

Serving: depends on the size of the cookie cutter

Prep Time: 5 to 10 minutes

Bake Time: 30 minutes

Total Time: 35 to 40 minutes

The list of ingredients:

- 1 large egg
- 2 ½ cups whole wheat or white flour
- 1/2 cup hot water

- 1 teaspoon salt
- 1 beef bouillon cube

Methods:

A. Preheat oven to 350-degrees. Line the bottom of a baking sheet with parchment paper. Set to the side for the moment.

B. Pour the water into a microwave-safe bowl. Heat the water in the microwave until it almost reaches the boiling point. Place the bouillon cube into the water and let dissolve completely. Stir the mixture once dissolved.

C. Place all the ingredients, including the beef broth from Step 2, into a mixing bowl. Mix until well combined.

D. Lightly flour your work surface and roll the dough out to a thickness of about ¼-inch.

E. Use your cookie cutter to cut the dough out and place on a single layer on the prepared baking sheet.

F. Bake the treats in the oven for 30 minutes. Once baked, remove from the oven, and let cool before transferring them to an airtight container.

9. Peanut Butter and Pumpkin Dog Treats

Serving: varies on the size of the cookie cutter

Prep Time: 20 to 25 minutes

Bake Time: 25 minutes

Total Time: 45 to 50 minutes

Ingredients:

- 2 large eggs (lightly beaten)
- 1/4 cup of creamy peanut butter

- 3 cups whole wheat flour + extra
- 2/3 cup pumpkin puree

Methods:

A. Preheat oven to 350 degrees. Line a baking sheet with a parchment paper. Set to the side for the moment.

B. Using a hand mixer, beat the peanut butter, pumpkin puree, and eggs together until smooth.

C. Gradually add in the 3 cups of whole wheat flour, a little at a time, until it is well incorporated.

D. Lightly cover a flat surface with some whole wheat flour. This will prevent the dough from sticking.

E. Roll the dough out on the floured surface to a thickness of about ¼-inch. Using the desired cookie cutter, cut the dough out before placing onto the prepared baking sheet from Step 1.

F. Bake the treats in the oven for 20 to 25 minutes. The treats are done when the edges have started to turn a golden-brown color.

G. Remove the baking sheet from the oven and transfer the treats to a cooling rack. Let cool completely before storing them in an airtight container.

10. Sweet Potato Pumpkin Bites

Serving: 100 to 120 treats

Prep Time: 5 to 10 minutes

Bake Time: 30 minutes

Total Time: 35 to 40 minutes

The list of ingredients:

- 1 ½ cups brown rice flour
- 1/2 cup pumpkin puree
- 2 tablespoons pure organic maple syrup
- 1/2 cup water

- 1 large egg
- 1 cup mashed sweet potato

Methods:

A. Preheat an oven to 350 degrees. Use parchment paper to line the bottoms of two baking sheets. Set to the side for the moment.

B. Mix the sweet potato, flour, pumpkin, maple syrup, egg, and water together until well combined.

C. Roll the dough into small ¾ teaspoon sized balls. Place the balls on the prepared baking sheet, making sure to keep them spaced apart.

D. Using a fork, press each ball down a bit to flatten them a little and leave behind fork marks.

E. Bake for 20 minutes with the baking sheet in the oven. Remove the baking sheet from the oven and carefully flip the goodies over. Return to the oven and bake for another 10 minutes.

F. Transfer the treats to a cooling rack and let cool completely. Store the treats in an airtight container in the fridge for up to 7 days.

11. Oats and Applesauce Carrot Treats

Serving: 10 to 14 treats

Prep Time: 10 minutes

Bake Time: 20 to 25 minutes

Total Time: 30 to 35 minutes

The list of ingredients

- 1/2 cup all-purpose flour
- 1/2 cup quick cooking oat

- 1/2 cup carrot (peeled and finely grated)
- 1/2 cup unsweetened applesauce

Methods:

A. Preheat oven to 350 degrees. Line the bottom of a baking sheet with a parchment paper. Set to the side for the moment.

B. Place all the ingredients in a mixing bowl and mix until well combined.

C. Drop the dough onto the prepared baking sheet from Step 1 by rounded tablespoons. Make sure to leave some space between each treat.

D. Place the baking sheet in the pre-heated oven and bake for about 20 to 25 minutes.

E. Remove the baking sheet from the oven and transfer the treats to a cooling rack. Let them cool completely before storing them in an airtight container.

Chapter 2 – Pupsicles for Your Pup: Frozen Dog Treat Recipes

12. Banana and Peanut Butter Frozen Dog Treats

Serving: 25 to 30

Total Time: 10 minutes to make + overnight to freeze

The list of ingredients:

- 1 cup
- 1/2 cup smooth peanut butter
- 2 bananas (overly ripe)

Methods:

A. Peel the bananas. Place the peeled bananas in a mixing bowl and mash until smooth. Add the yogurt and peanut butter. Mix until all three ingredients are well combined and smooth.

B. Transfer the mixture into the desired molds. Place the molds in the freezer and freeze overnight.

C. Pop the treats out of the mold and store in an airtight container or freezer bag. When ready to use, remove a treat from the storage container and give to your pooch.

13. Peanutty Bacon and Carroty Banana Pupsicles

Serving: 6 to 10 treats

Total Time: 2 hours 5 minutes + several hours to freeze

The list of ingredients:

- 6 ripe bananas (peeled)
- 3 tablespoons peanut butter (creamy)
- 1/2 cup carrot (peeled and shredded)
- 2 bacon slices (cooked and crumbled)

Methods:

A. Slice the bananas into disks that measure about ½-inch thick. Place them in a freezer bag and set in the freezer for about 2 hours or until they are frozen.

B. Dump the frozen banana slices into a blender or food processor. Pulse until the bananas are smooth. It should have a consistency similar to soft serve ice cream.

C. Blend in the peanut butter until well incorporated. Fold in the cooked bacon crumbles and the shredded carrots.

D. Transfer the mixture into the desired molds and place in the freezer. Freeze for several hours until completely frozen.

E. Remove the treats from the mold and store in an airtight container in the freezer.

14. Yogurt and Watermelon Frozen Treats

Serving: 15 to 30 treats

Total Time: 5 minutes to make + 4 hours to freeze

The list of ingredients:

- 1 cup plain yogurt
- 2 cups seedless diced watermelon

Methods:

A. Blend the watermelon in a blender or food processor until smooth.

B. Place about 1 tablespoon of yogurt into each opening of the mold.

C. Fill the remaining space of the mold with the pureed watermelon.

D. Place the treats in the freezer and let freeze for 4 hours.

E. Once frozen, remove the treats from the mold and store in a freezer bag or airtight container.

15. Banana Pumpkin Dog Pops

Serving: 6 to 10

Total Time: 5 minutes + overnight to freeze

The list of ingredients:

- 15 ounces pumpkin puree
- 1 ripe banana (peeled)
- 1 teaspoon organic honey
- 1 cup plain yogurt (non-fat)

Methods:

A. Place the peeled banana and pumpkin puree into a food processor. Pulse until the mixture is smooth. Transfer the mixture to a mixing bowl.

B. Add the yogurt into the banana mixture and mix until well combined. Stir in the honey.

C. Press the mixture into the desired molds and set in the freezer. Freeze overnight.

D. Pop the frozen treats out of the mold and into an airtight container. Store in the freezer until ready to use.

16. Banana and Strawberry Frozen Smoothie Dog Treats

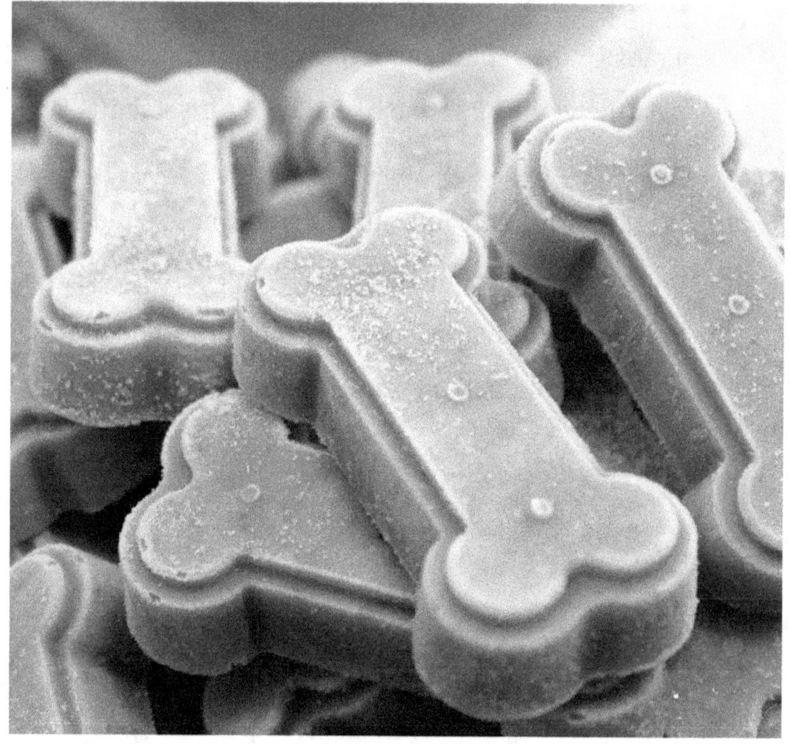

Serving: Depends on the mold

Total Time: 10 minutes + 4 or more hours to freeze

The list of ingredients:

- 1 banana, peeled and sliced

- 1 ½ cups low-fat Greek yogurt (plain)
- 1/4 cup skim milk
- 2 cups strawberries (destemmed and sliced)
- 3 tablespoons honey

Methods:

A. Put all the ingredients into a blender. On medium speed, blend the mixture for several minutes until smooth.

B. Pour the blended mixture into the desired molds. Molds shaped like a bone work great, but any mold will do.

C. Place the mold in the freezer and let freeze for at least 4 hours.

D. Once the treats are completely frozen, pop them out of the mold. Store the treats in an airtight container or Ziploc bag in the freezer. With proper storage, these treats can be stored for up to 2 months.

17. Blueberry Pupsicles

Serving: 4 to 8

Total Time: 5 minutes + 4 or more hours to freeze

The list of ingredients:

- 1 cup washed and dried blueberries
- 16 ounces plain yogurt (non-fat)

Methods:

A. Place the yogurt and the blueberries into a blender

and blend. Divide the mixture between 4 to 8 miniature Dixie cups. You can simply freeze them as is, or insert a stick in the middle for supervised consuming.

B. Place the Dixie cups in the freezer and freeze for at least 4 hours. Store the unused pupsicles in the freezer until ready to feed to your dog.

18. Apple and Chicken Broth Frozen Treats

Serving: 25 to 50, depending on the mold used

Total Time: 10 minutes to make + 4 or more hours to freeze

The list of ingredients:

- 32 ounces organic chicken broth
- 1 ½ pounds cored and sliced apples

Methods:

A. Prepare the apple slices by chopping them into bite-sized pieces.

B. Divide the prepared apples between an ice tray or Jell-O shot container.

C. Fill each ice tray opening or container with the chicken broth, making sure to leave a small amount of room at the top. If using a Jell-O shot container, secure the lid onto it before continuing.

D. Freeze the treats in the freezer for at least 4 hours.

E. Once frozen, remove the ice tray from the freezer and pop the treats out. Store in an airtight container or Ziploc bag in the freezer. Jell-O shot containers can stay in the freezer until ready to use.

19. Coconut Oil and Peanut Butter Frozen Dog Treats

Serving: depends on the mold

Total Time: 10 minutes to make + 4 or more hours to freeze

The list of ingredients:

- 1 teaspoon ground cinnamon
- 1 tablespoon coconut oil (unprocessed)
- 1 cup peanut butter (smooth and all-natural)

Methods:

A. Melt the coconut oil in a saucepan over medium heat. Once the coconut oil is completely melted, remove from heat.

B. Stir the peanut butter into the melted coconut oil until smooth. Add the cinnamon. Mix until all three ingredients are well combined.

C. Transfer the mixture into the desired molds and freeze for 4 or more hours.

D. Once frozen, pop the treats out of the molds and place in a freezer bag or airtight container. Store in the freezer for up to 2 months.

Chapter 3 – Eww, Doggie Breath: Homemade Breath Fresheners for Your Pooch

20. Minty Oat Breath Freshener for Dogs

Serving: 35 to 40 mints

Prep Time: 10 minutes

Bake Time: 35 to 40 minutes

Total Time: 45 to 50 minutes

The list of ingredients:

- 1/4 cup unsweetened applesauce

- 2 ½ cups old-fashioned oats
- 1/4 cup + 1 teaspoon water
- 1/2 cup fresh chopped finely mint
- 3 tablespoons coconut oil
- 1/2 cup fresh chopped finely parsley

Methods:

A. Preheat oven to 325 degrees. Line a baking or cookie sheet with parchment paper. Set to the side for the moment.

B. Pulse the oats in a blender or food processor until they have a consistency similar to flour. Set to the side for the moment.

C. Whisk the applesauce, coconut oil, water, mint, and parsley together in a mixing bowl.

D. Add the oat flour from Step 2 into the mixture from Step 3 and knead with your hands until well combined. Avoid over-kneading.

E. Turn the dough out onto a floured surface. Using a rolling pin, roll the dough out to a thickness of about 1/8-inch.

F. Using a cookie cutter, cut the dough into 1-inch circles. Set the circles onto the prepared sheet from

Step 1, leaving about ¼-inch between each mint.

G. Bake the dough in the preheated oven for 35 to 40 minutes. You want the mints to be crispy and golden.

H. Remove the mints from the oven and let cool completely before storing in an airtight container.

21. Chicken Peas and Herbs Doggy Breath Treats

Serving: 8 to 10 treats

Prep Time: 10 minutes

Bake Time: 30 to 35 minutes

Total Time: 40 to 45 minutes

The list of ingredients:

- 1/2 cup fresh chopped coarsely parsley
- 1 can drained and rinsed chickpeas
- Silicon oven-safe mold (bone-shaped)
- 1/2 cup chopped coarsely fresh mint
- 1 large egg

Methods:

A. Preheat oven to 350 degrees.

B. Place all the ingredients into a food processor or blender. Pulse until the mixture is smooth and well incorporated into one another.

C. Press the mixture into the oven-safe mold. Place the mold in the preheated oven and bake for 35 to 40 minutes. Remember that the smaller the mold, the less time it takes to bake. You want the breath freshening treats to be crispy and starting to brown on the top.

D. Remove the mold from the oven and carefully pop the treats out. Set the treats on a cooling rack and let cool completely.

E. Store the treats in an airtight container for up to a week.

22. Frosty Dog Breath Treats

Serving: 10 to 14 treats

Total Time: 10 minutes to make + 6 hours to freeze

The list of ingredients:

- 1/2 cup plain Greek yogurt
- 1/2 cup fresh mint
- 1/2 cup coconut oil
- 1/2 cup fresh parsley
- 1/2 cup chicken broth that doesn't contain onion

Methods:

A. Warm the chicken broth on the stove before pouring it into a blender or food processor. Add in the coconut oil and pulse until the mixture is smooth.

B. Add the yogurt, parsley, and mint, and continue to blend until all the ingredients are smooth and well combined.

C. Transfer the mixture into the desired molds and place in the freezer. Let freeze for at least 6 hours.

D. Once frozen, remove the treats from the molds and into an airtight container. Store in the freezer.

23. Homemade Dog Breath Fresheners

Serving: depends on the cookie cutter

Prep Time: 5 to 10 minutes

Bake Time: 20 to 25 minutes

Total Time: 25 to 35 minutes + drying time

The list of ingredients:

- 1/4 cup fresh parsley
- 1 cup water

- 3 cups oat flour

- 1/4 cup fresh mint

- 1 cup coconut flour

- 1/4 cup coconut oil

- 2 large eggs (lightly beaten)

Methods:

A. Prep the mint and parsley by cutting and discarding the stems of the fresh herbs. You only want to use the leafy parts. Set the prepared herbs to the side for the moment.

B. Preheat the oven to 350 degrees. Line the bottom of 2 baking sheets with parchment paper and set to the side for the moment.

C. In a large mixing bowl, stir together the coconut flour and the oat flour. Mix in the prepared mint and parsley from Step 1.

D. Stir in the water, eggs, and coconut oil until well combined. Using your hands, knead the dough into a solid ball. If you find that they dough is too crumbly to form a ball, add 1 tablespoon of water at a time until it achieves the right consistency.

E. Roll the dough out onto a lightly floured surface to a thickness of about ¼-inch.

F. Cut the dough out using the desired cookie cutters. Bone-shaped cookie cutters work well but any shape will do.

G. Transfer the cut dough onto the prepared baking sheet, making sure to leave a bit of space between each treat.

H. Place the baking sheet in the oven and bake for 20 to 25 minutes. After the allotted time, turn the oven off but leave the baking sheets in the oven until they dry out. Once completely cooled, remove the baking sheets from the oven.

I. Store the treats in an airtight container. They will last up to 2 weeks at room temperature or 2 months in the freezer.

24. Fresh Breath Dog Treats

Serving: 10 to 15 treats

Total Time: 10 minutes to make + 1 hour to chill

The list of ingredients:

- 1/4 cup chopped fresh mint
- 1 ½ cups softened coconut oil
- Turmeric
- 1/2 cup chopped fresh parsley

Methods:

A. Place the softened coconut oil into a mixing bowl. Mix in the finely chopped parsley and mint until well combined.

B. Roll the mixture into small balls. You want them to be bite-sized so choose a size that would work best for your dog.

C. Place the balls on a baking sheet lined with parchment paper.

D. Sprinkle some turmeric over top each ball. Set the baking sheet in the fridge and let chill for about an hour.

E. Transfer the chilled breath freshening treats to an airtight container. Store in the fridge when not using.

25. Doggie Breath Mints

Serving: 80 to 100 treats

Prep Time: 10 to 15 minutes

Bake Time: 25 minutes

Total Time: 35 to 40 minutes

The list of ingredients:

- 2 ½ cups all-purpose flour
- 3/4 cup reduced fat milk

- 1 tablespoon baking soda

- 2 large eggs

- 1/2 cup fresh peppermint

- 1 cup smooth peanut butter

- 1/2 cup fresh basil

Methods:

A. Preheat oven to 325 degrees. Line the bottom of a baking sheet with parchment paper. Set to the side for the moment.

B. In a large bowl, whisk together the egg, milk, and smooth peanut butter until well blended.

C. Mix in the flour and baking soda until just combined. You want to avoid overmixing.

D. Roughly chop the fresh peppermint and basil before folding it into the dough.

E. Roll the dough out onto a floured surface so that it has a thickness of about ¼-inch. Using a small 2-inch circle cookie cutter, cut the dough out and set on the prepared baking sheet from Step 1.

F. Whisk the remaining egg with 2 teaspoons of water. Thinly brush the egg wash over the treats.

G. Bake the treats in the oven for 15 minutes. Carefully flip the treats over. Thinly brush the egg wash on the opposite side before placing the treats bake into the oven for 10 minutes.

H. Remove the baking sheet from the oven and transfer the treats to a cooling rack. Let the treats completely cool before transferring them to an airtight container.

I. Store the treats in your airtight container for up to 7 days at room temperature or 2 months in the freezer.